Camel for a King

WRITTEN AND ILLUSTRATED BY
Penelope Beach Chittenden

PAULIST PRESS • NEW YORK/MA

Copyright © 1996 by Penelope Beach Chittenden

All rights reserved. No part of this book may be reproduced or transmitted in any form or by any means, electronic or mechanical, including photocopying, recording or any information storage and retrieval system without permission in writing from the Publisher.

Library of Congress Cataloging-in-Publication Data

Chittenden, Penelope.
  Camel for a king / written and illustrated by Penelope Beach Chittenden.
    p. cm.
  Summary: After being banished for chewing on everything in sight, a young camel makes a lonely journey across the desert and meets up with three kings who take her along to see a special baby.
  ISBN 0-8091-6633-X (alk. paper)
  [1. Camels—Fiction. 2. Jesus Christ—Nativity—Fiction.]
I. Title.
PZ7.C44525Cam 1996
[E]—dc20
                                                               96-5416
                                                                   CIP
                                                                      AC

Published by Paulist Press
997 Macarthur Boulevard
Mahwah, New Jersey 07430

Printed and bound in the United States of America

Designed by James F. Brisson, Williamsville, VT

For my five daughters and five grandchildren
who nurture the child in me
and keep wonder alive.

Mia was born in the hot dry desert. She lived with her mother, father, aunts, uncles and forty cousins. They were all part of Abdul's camel train.

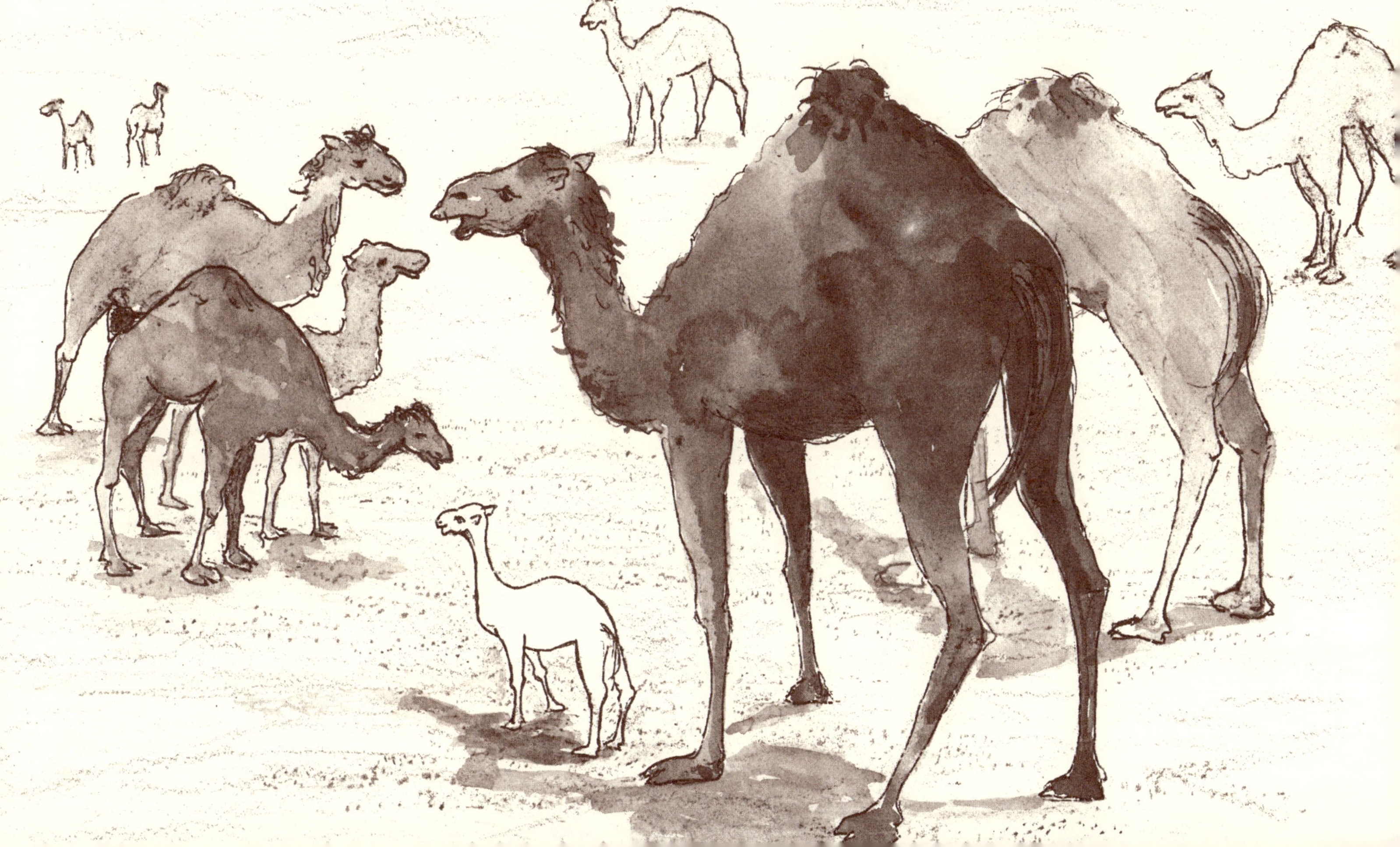

She had plenty of camel milk to drink, but Mia was always hungry. There was nothing much to eat in the desert. She nibbled Abdul's tent.

Abdul said, "STOP! Stop chewing my tent."

He shouted at the little camel, "Quit now or you can't stay here."

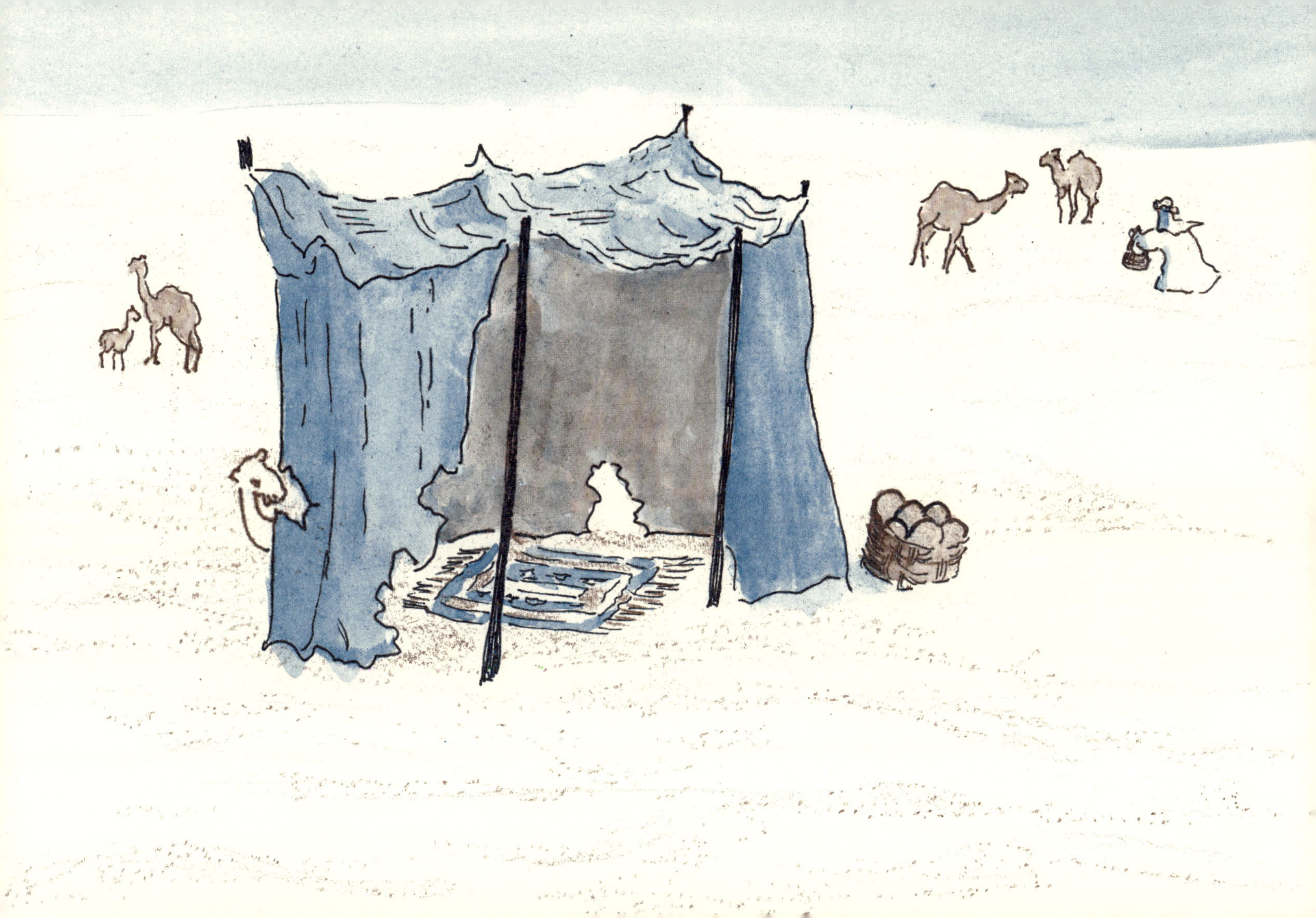

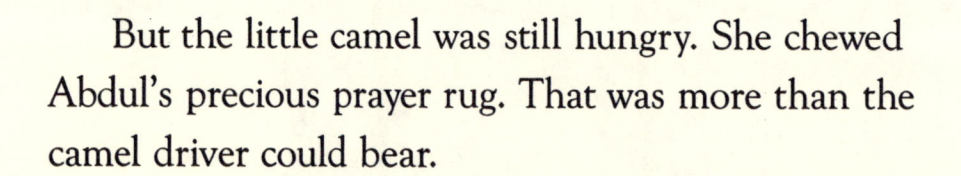

But the little camel was still hungry. She chewed Abdul's precious prayer rug. That was more than the camel driver could bear.

"Get out. GO. Away with you," he screamed at Mia.

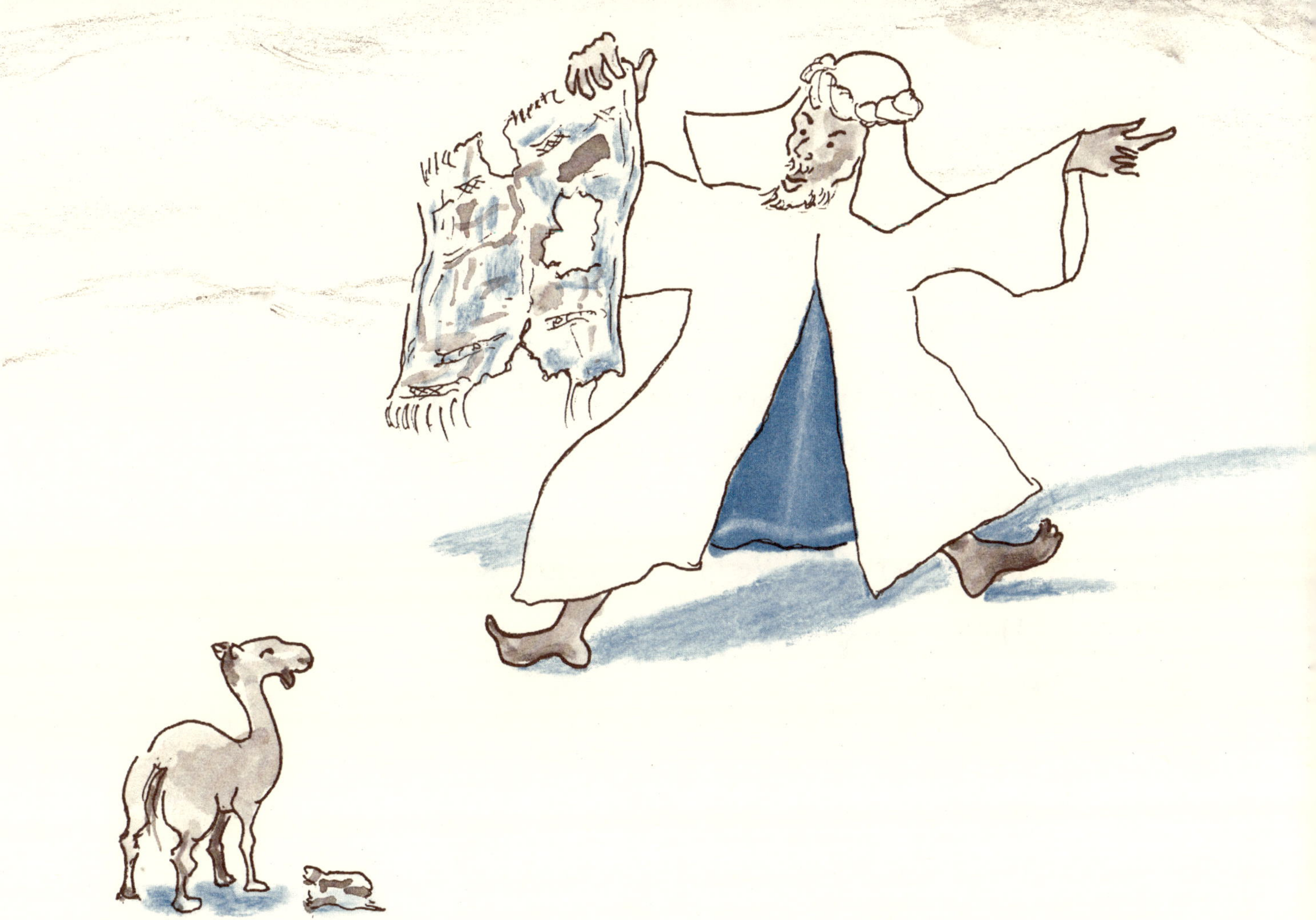

Mia was very sad. She blinked back a tear as her mother nuzzled her. Her forty cousins crowded around her.

Her father said, "Be brave, my little Mia."

Her uncles said, "Go east, Mia, to the Great River."

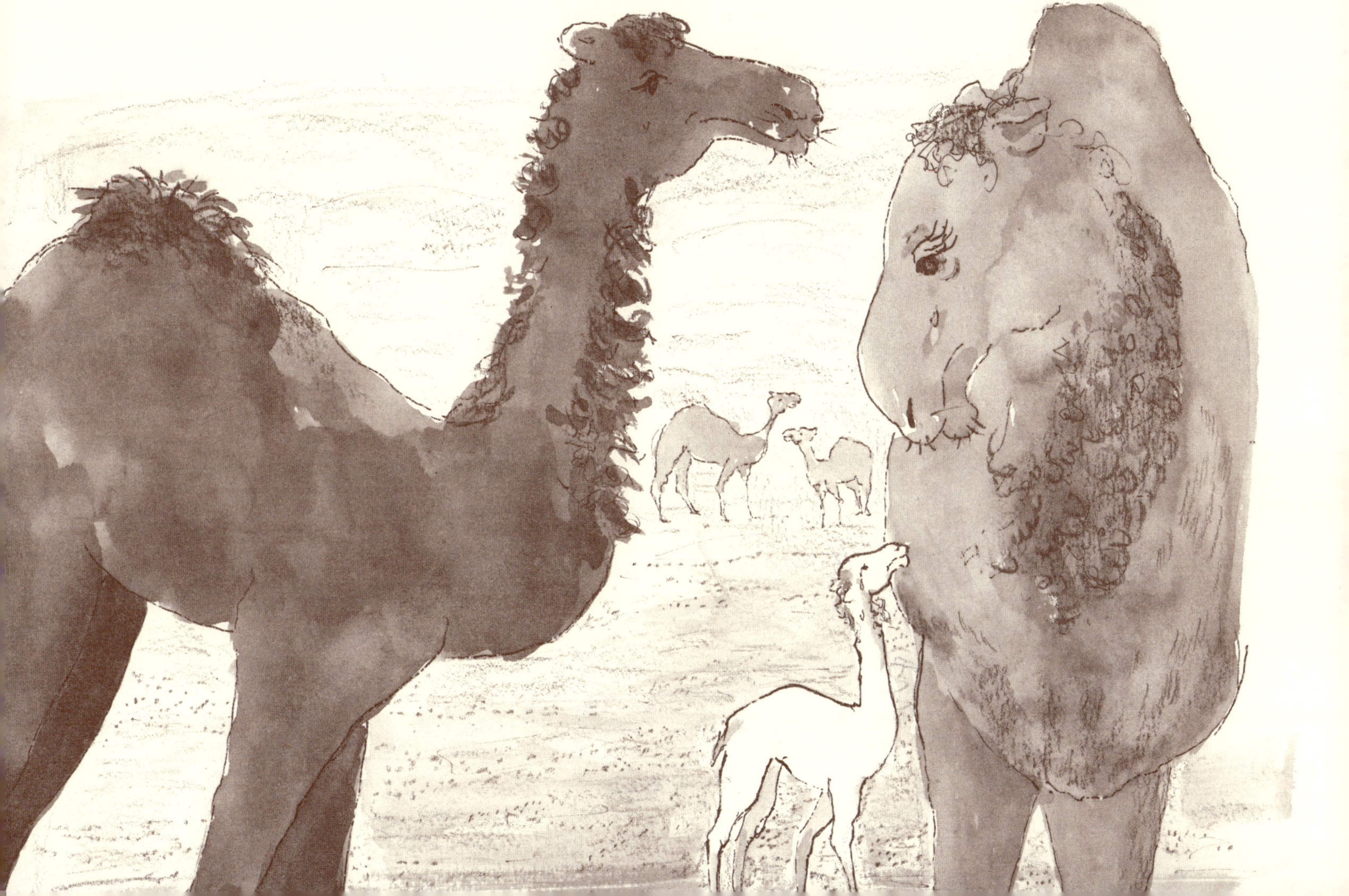

For three days Mia plodded across the hot dry desert.

The wind blew sand in her face and she had nothing to eat.

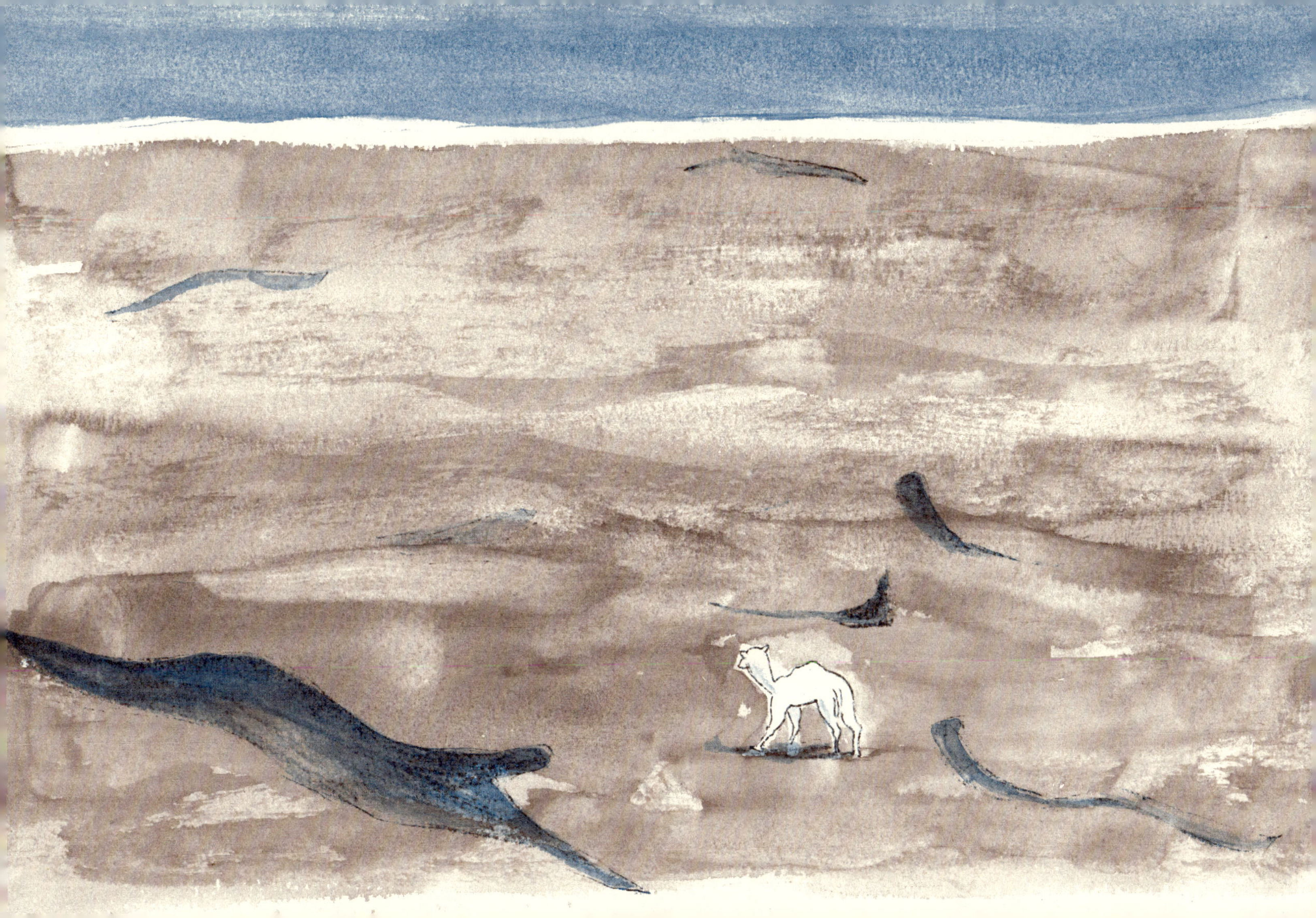

Finally she reached the banks of the Nile River. At first she wondered what it was, for she had never seen water.

Here she drank and drank the sweet, cool water.

Never had she seen trees and plants like these. She tasted a leaf, and then another and another. Mia ate many green leaves. Each day she grew bigger and stronger.

"This is a nice place to live," she thought.

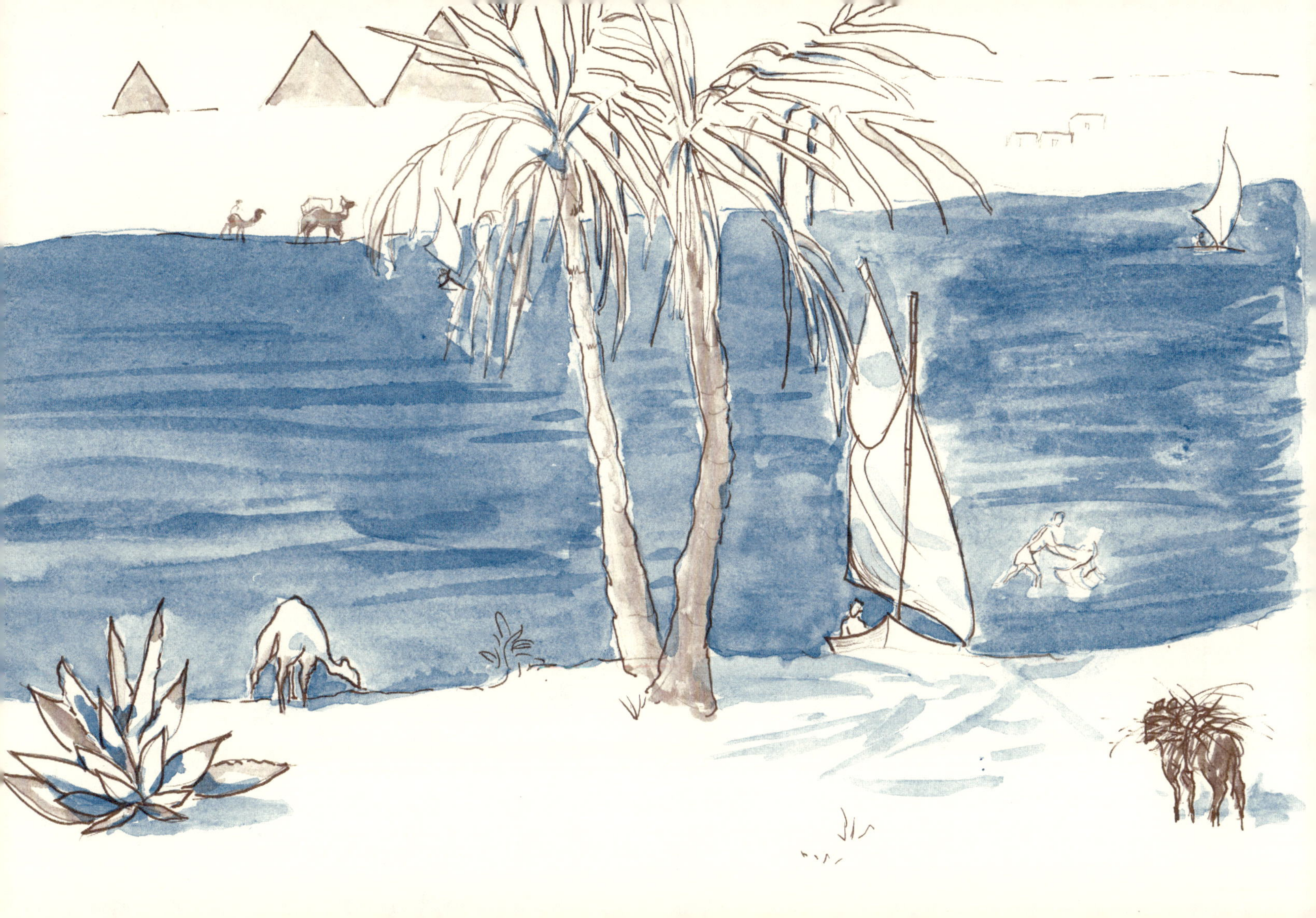

She saw pyramids, palaces, and many people. She also saw camels and donkeys carrying heavy loads on their backs. Mia did not want to do that.

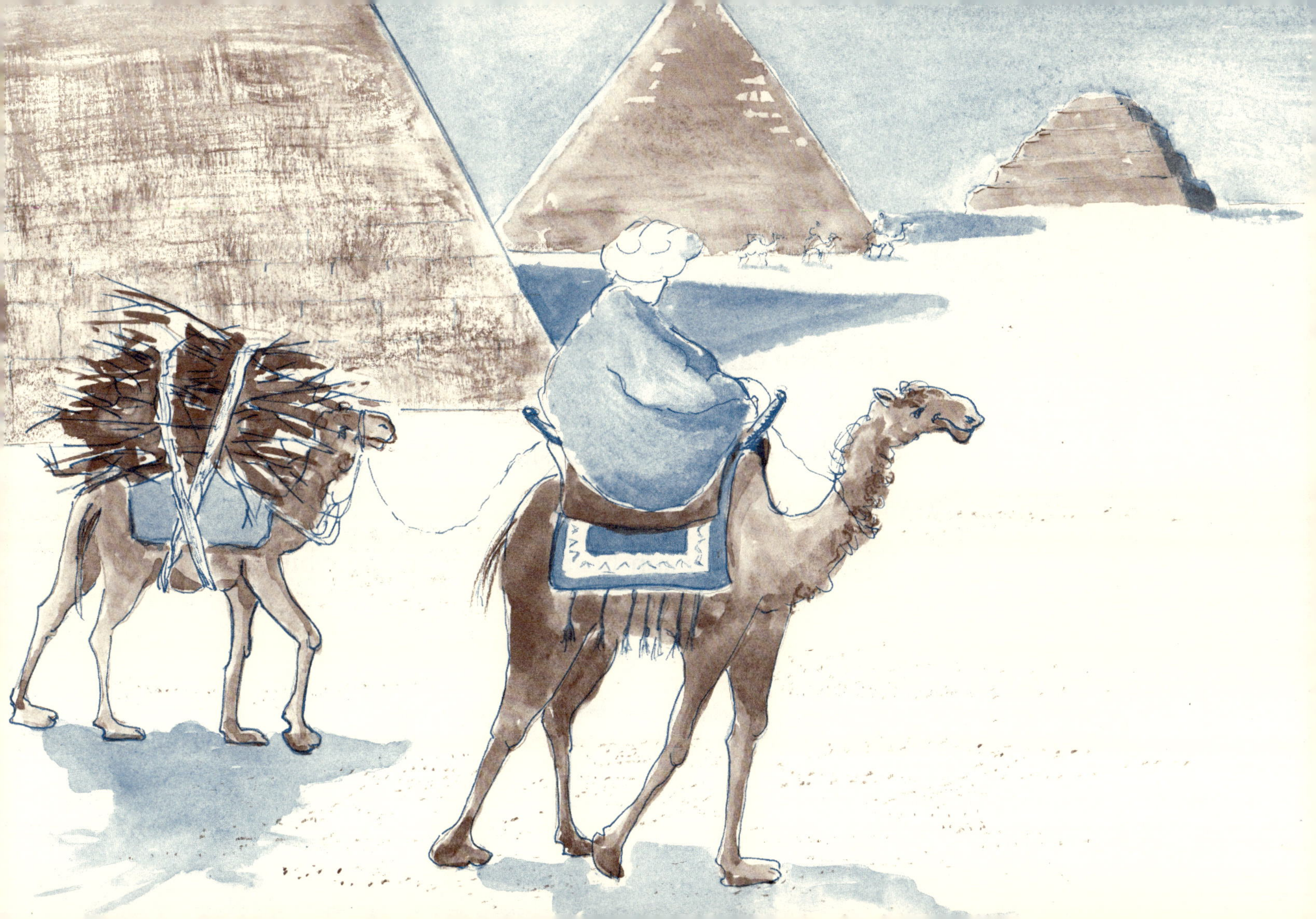

The little camel traveled along the banks of the river, eating all she could, until she came to shallow water. She crossed the river to the other side and kept going east toward the morning star.

The hot midday sun beat down upon the white sand.

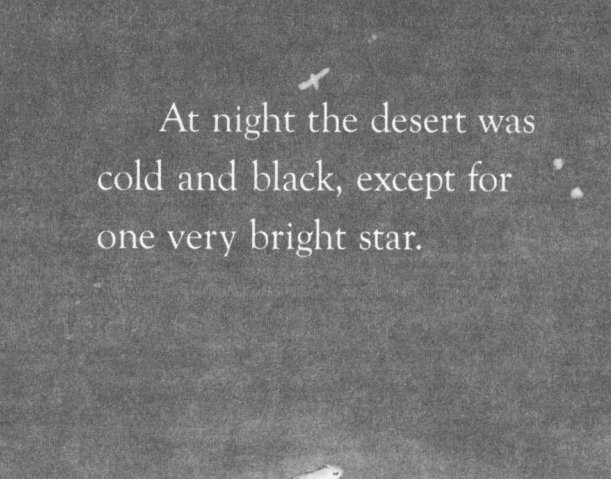

At night the desert was cold and black, except for one very bright star.

Eventually the tired little camel came to a wadi. A stream of clear water rose out of the sand, forming a long pool. Trees grew around it. In the welcome shade of a palm tree Mia lay down and fell fast asleep.

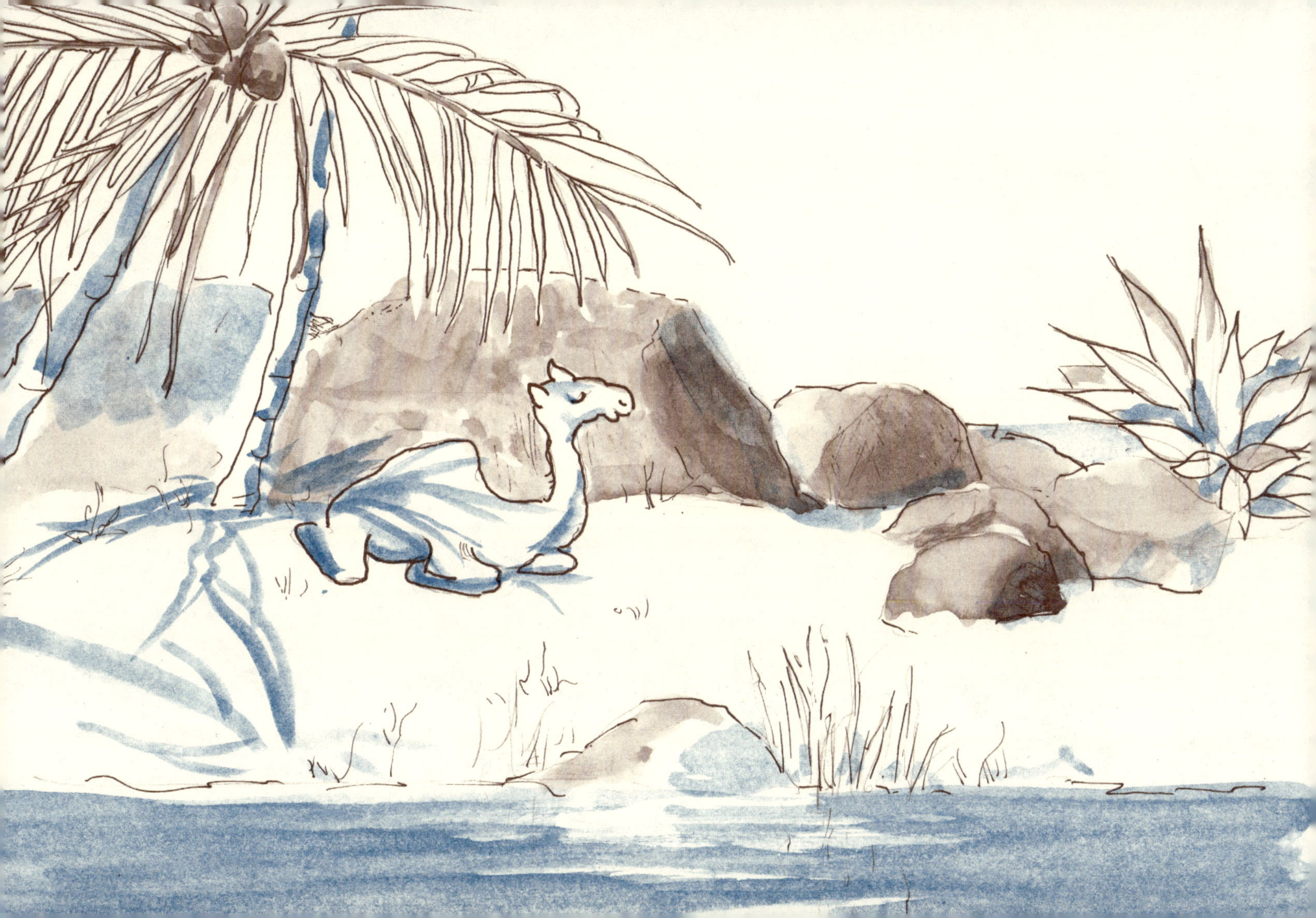

While Mia slept, a caravan of men and camels traveling from the east stopped to rest at the wadi. But as soon as the star rose again in the sky, the three men leading the caravan prepared to move on.

"Bring her along with the other camels," the tallest leader said to his camel driver.

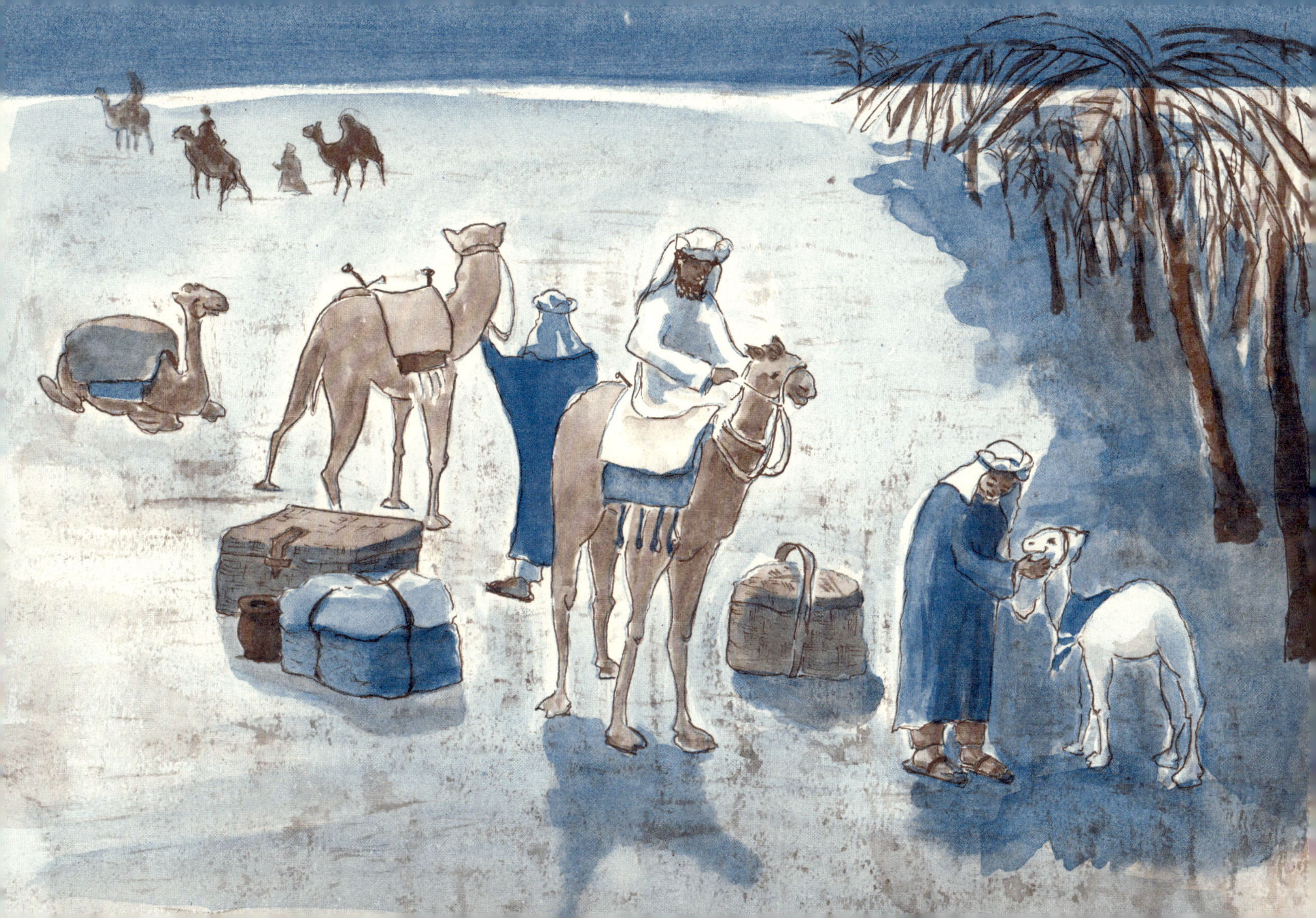

Mia was happy to carry a light load on her back. She liked being with the other camels.

Many days later the caravan halted outside a stable. The three men donned their finest robes and crowns. They looked very regal. Then they walked over to Mia and led the surprised little camel into the stable.

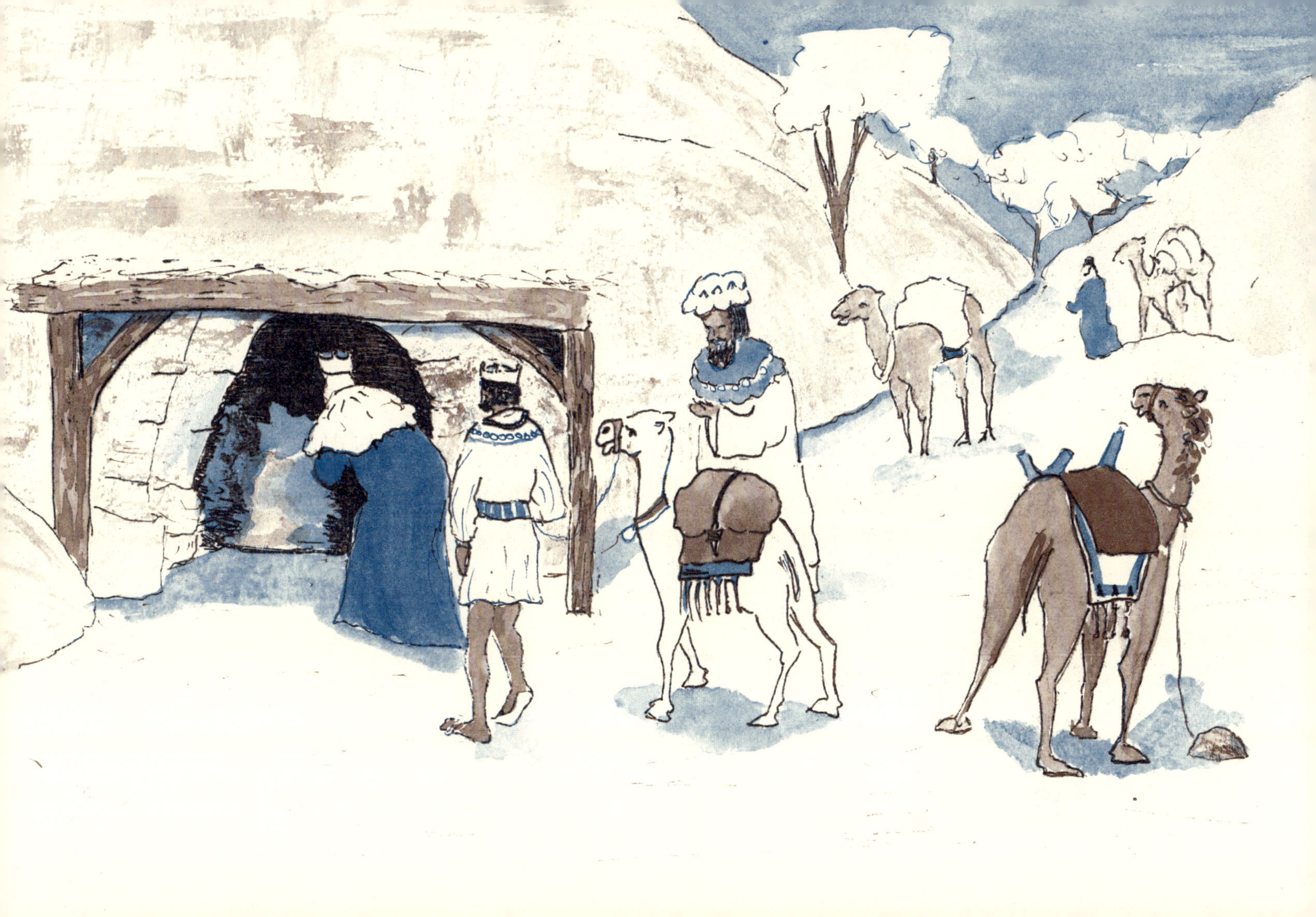

Mia saw the most beautiful sight she had ever seen. A man knelt beside a beautiful young woman who held a tiny baby in her arms. Around them lay lambs and an ox in silence.

Mia could not resist stretching her neck out to pull a piece of straw from the manger before lying down next to a lamb. The baby watched her nibble a straw.

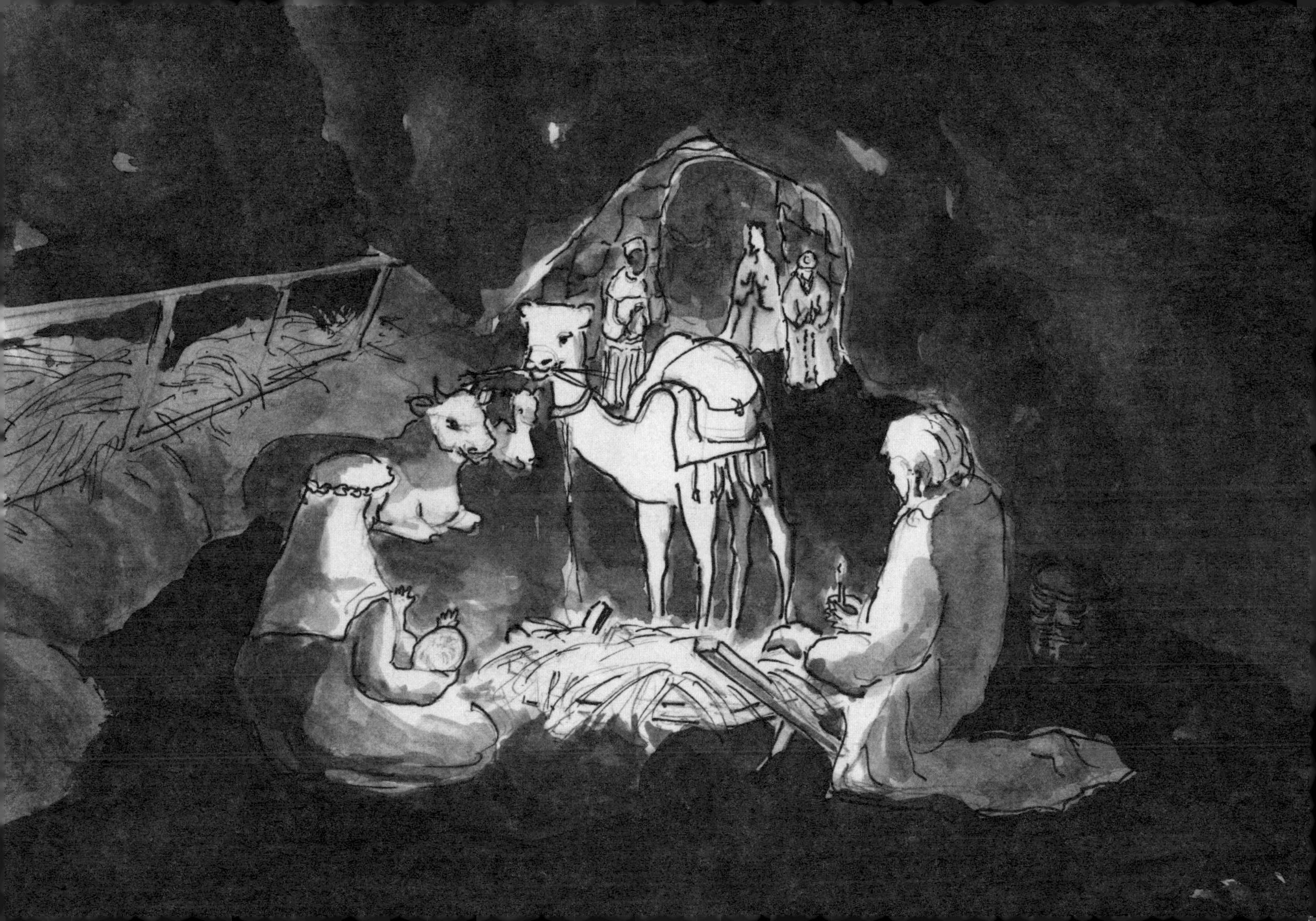

The kings removed the load from Mia's back and lay three precious boxes in front of the mother and child. One box was made of ivory. One box was made of gold and jewels. The third box was made of fine dark wood and silver.

"In these vessels are our gifts to your son," they declared. "Gold, frankincense, and myrrh."

The mother smiled.

"If you can spare her," she said, "my son would like the little camel who bore the gifts to him."

So with great joy, Mia stayed with the family. When the time came for the father to take the baby and his mother out of that country, Mia led them and their donkey to safety along the path she remembered, to the land by the banks of the Nile.

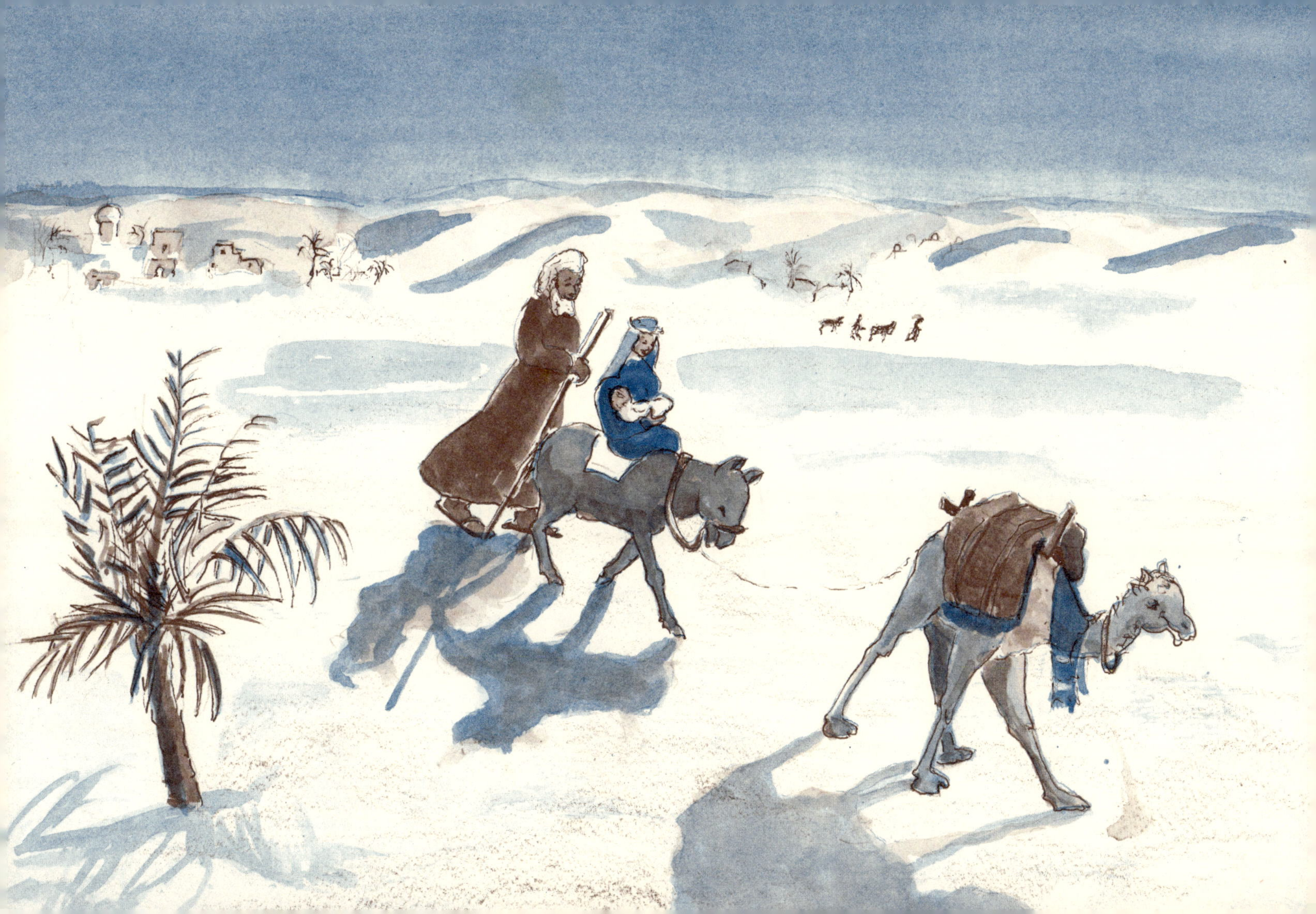

And there Mia dwelt for the rest of her days, living peacefully among the northern stars.